LASTING
LEAVING
LEFT

by Robin Dyke

PROMONTORY
P R E S S

Promontory Press
www.promontorypress.com

ISBN: 978-1-987857-20-7

Cover design by Marla Thompson of Edge of Water Designs
Typeset by One Owl Creative in 11pt Garamond Premier Pro

Printed in Canada
0987654321

Lasting
Leaving
Left

Accompanied on the journey ...

Live by the harmless untruths that make you
brave and kind and healthy and happy.

– The Books of Bokonon
(*Cat's Cradle*, Kurt Vonnegut, Jr.)

More Bokononism – Humanity is believed to be organized into teams that do God's will without ever discovering what they are doing. Such a team is called a *karass* (little did you suspect your complicity in this collection of poems).

About *my karass*, then:

Marline – for just believing
Mom and Dad – for my being
My Grandfather – for all the early depth of meanings
Mike and Yana – for encouraging first revealings

Judy and Hanne – for reflective picnicking

Tom – for potting and painting

Yvonne – for untiring 'tighten' and 'push the image'

KR – for disruptive spark

… and all the others of whom I am oblivious to your kindness
and support.

Nice, nice, very nice –
so many different people
to push my vice

Contents

Lasting

What is it that's blest, that endures?

When can a sock not look like a sock and

still be a sock?

– with apologies to James Hillman

Picnic

Three friends spread a woven blanket
frayed and patched with years between
Lay out stories as picnic plates
filled with carrot, broccoli, a mother's death
salsa, baked quiche, another parent's care
homemade rakija, a ladder fall, ambitions quelled
birthday cake, candles of laughter amid - oh really!

Bounty mellowed by an autumn sun
an unhurried tide
Crow and seagull caws and squawks
stitched within the conversation
Some ends stay loose, some are tied
A fish boat points out to sea
Waves of sharing ebb
Confession flows to contemplation
Afternoon's lengthening shadow
tugging at the edges of each other's worlds

Time - pack up, tuck
threads back in with care -
a weave more languid stored

Life

By seed, by birth
    breath, cry, cling
By night, by day
    dream, crave, wonder
By growth, by age
    play, stretch, stumble
By school, by work
    learn, create, give back
By marriage, by divorce
    love, fall, rebound
By children, by grandchildren
    nurture, anguish, set free
By hook, win/lose
    by crook, grieve/deny
By peace, accept;
    yet question
By light, more light
    to shadow, to dark
To all, from nothing
    start to end –
An egg, one sperm
    all begins again

The Donut's Whole

Whatever be your goal, keep your eye upon
the donut and not upon the hole

- Downyflake Donut Shop
Toronto, circa 1950

Tempus fugit the ancients warned
picks up speed each passing year
At the outset, time limitless and full
like vacations or overflowing draft of beer
Abundance, volume, endless fame
shifts to what's gone not what remains
As if it's time's reign that's running out
rather than our view of what we are about
Lost the lesson of the soul
eyes here now upon the whole

Goals

Some claim goals
are good, some
laugh them off

Strange enough
in have or not
we've made a goal
along with our bed

What's not in a goal
that's in our dreams?
And what of what
that's in between?

By any means or ends
is lived choice not
the mirror of the reach
we've sought?

Hunger

Outside of routine
our soul camps patiently
panhandling for meaning
Startled, we turn aside
step hastily away

Star Bright

What's in our stars, a universe away –
an aura caught at early age
Reminder with each passing stage
as one's uniqueness fades more each day
Despair will be the price you pay
to keep high hopes stuffed in a cage
Go not into dark night quietly with no rage
there will be time eternal just to lay
Why hesitation, why self-restraint?
Ask more of yourself than easy rent
It's you who you will have for complaint
to miss the call sweet destiny has sent
Pursue your dreams, *someday* is too late
fire up your stars, reignite your fate

Love Affair

... and I grew up

fostered alike by beauty and by fear.

– Wordsworth

War and violence are human things
harbored deep within mythic roots

The gods' warring passions sing
entrap us willingly in their hold

Sublime, kept darkly out of sight
beneath the lamb, rage always bold
tiger burning brightest for love of fight

With Mars and Ares ever here to stay
a terrible love of war is in our seed
Inhuman chaos at its worst –
Chechnya, Bosnia or Iraq
Syria, Afghanistan, no turning back
No chance that might itself
will ever mitigate such brutal thirst
(even the gods themselves cannot reverse)

Robin Dyke

Hope's false face attempts a ruse
as if lines exist between love and war
Even pale Venus is caught in the bed
of savage Mars their attraction paired

A terrible love of war conflicts our deeds

Lance

Once what was,
was to be like Lance
kick-assing each moment
no preoccupation with tomorrow's plans
Today is all I have
Remission clears lethargic haze
what's to hold back – ride, fly!
Do or not do is all there is
(clear choice – do or not do dope as well)
In do, grow down, or fall
from wings of wax
Truth speaks truth
on how you reach your heights
melts Icarus illusions
back to earth,
or into dirt

Robin Dyke

In Passing

On any path
do you smile, nod,
brightly say good-day?
Or do you just pass
eyes straight ahead?
Perhaps a quick glance
before your eyes avert
or look to the ground?
Or are you prone
to be simply lost
in pressing thought?
Why not -- play a different tune
of presence with those you pass?
A possibility of Goldberg variations
on the human scale
hello!

Silly

Franklin called his sister stupid
Not nice! Mom said
silly must be used instead
But mouths of babes, so much more lucid
she's - Stupid! Stupid! Stupid!

Robin Dyke

Certain Uncertainty

The truth as certainty is illusion
If all seems clear you've misunderstood
What you heard is not what was meant
What you believe you will repent

If all seems clear you've misunderstood
Facts withheld so hard to tell
What you heard is not what was meant
To protect uncertainty truth gets bent

Facts withheld so hard to tell
Mystery not transparency is what you get
To protect uncertainty truth gets bent
So what can be believed when trust is spent?

Mystery not transparency is what you get
What you heard is not what was meant
What can be believed when trust is spent?
The truth -- certainly is born illusion

Check Out

The bagger
appeared detached from
connection, his
indifferent eyes
sought only the cashier's attention
as he strained forward
over the back of the check-out
At that instant
my glance struck
braces on spindly
undeveloped legs
First impression crushed
on the rock pile
strewn with judgment's
easy haste

Robin Dyke

Flight

Mid-way between San Salvador & Vancouver
thinking of an ailing friend

I flew over Denver
last night
A kindred spirit
far beyond
the city's bright
bravado, radiating up
to inky darkness, spread
far beyond
Knowing somewhere below
within the sprinkle
of isolated lights
the shadow on your life
creeps
My gesture to reach out
beyond
life and death
So distanced
you on the ground
me at heights unbound

I flew far above your door
wished -
the angel of the night could
make all things right

Invitation

My working out
attracted his canine sense of play
Bee-lined for me
Dropped his glistening ball
as invitation
Sensing hesitation, picked it up
dropped it closer
Come on! his hairs bristled
I kept to my jumping jacks
Not satisfied, this time
closer, right before my moving feet
His energy radiated
anticipation of the chase
Stoically I held my routine
No fun left in this guy!
Snatched up his offering
gone, as quickly
as he sought my company

Ties

I say family matters.
Really?
Of course, blood binds all.
To what, self suffrage -
as brother's keeper,
a coat of dreams worn by guilt?
Really!
So cold and harsh!
No more than sacrificial sons.
My point has been missed.
As brother's keeper,
not missed by clan or sect.
You take this to extremes!
Really!
My point but for their ends.
I give up!
As holy ghost you can't,
in your heart you know -
it's people who matter most.
Truly.

Robin Dyke

Mom & I

Twenty years more or less -
the spread of our ages
narrowing
Your bloom wears kindly
in winter's lengthening shadows;
my highway restless spring -
hills beyond hills calling

Grandfather

No doubt he shaped me from the start
as first grandchild I won his heart
A kind face grizzled more than saintly
his affections my first recollections

My early years with him on the loose
riding his handlebars to the Y
trolling salmon in his rowboat off Nanoose
Prepping his pipe or lapped with a dog
to my stories he was all-agog
Quick with Latin quip to draw a lesson
(*cogitabo pro te* - think for yourself)
or poetic line a drama lessen
(...*were scrapped to death with oyster shells*)
- life in the moment was revealed
 in new light and opened up

Loyal to his origins, served in wars
prayed each morning to his God
Adventure second nature to his being
climbed the pyramids, surveyed
the prairies' furthest reachings
Small pleasures he took in little things

Robin Dyke

tending nasturtiums or to take a swim
Without question at his core
humility, manners, humor –
all easy presences that he wore
A remarkable man in so many ways
wonder for him in each day

Ever seeking news of my world
connection the compass to his bearing
His letters entertained, enticed
the substance of his writing had no price;
themed with encouragement and care
self-deprecating incidents of his chores
and countless dogs from pounds he spared
When later self-absorbed my visits strayed
any judgment on his part was stayed
After death sent reassurance
not to fret, by dream forgave

The steady lettering of his hand –
from GRANDFATHER
guardian of my soul and brand

Father & Son Communion

Oh how I miss my dad
My father pleaded out like random thought
Or so it seemed as if he had

His manner and his voice were sad
Melancholy bore the comfort sought
Oh how I miss my dad

A switch to confession how he felt bad
That my blond boyhood hair was Olsen lot
Or so it seemed as if he had

Jealousy of my uncle he did add
So between his love and ego I was caught
Oh how I miss my dad

As quickly as his heart came unclad
To something else he spun off about
Or so it seemed as if he ever had

Subject to his King Lear gone mad
I might have shook him with a shout
How *I* miss *my* dad!
Or so it seemed I wish I had

Love Off The Shelf

Too late now to accept
your administrative reaching out –
your show of order
last bequests, tidily arranged
three hole punched documents
Your plots and plans
laid out and shelved
as dust will go to dust
you'd put all right
Me expecting more connection
missed what you were offering
as was your way
missed your point completely
That I could have acknowledged
this - at least!
But no, my impatience overran
this and other unsaid truths;
the biggest that *I loved you*,
along with appreciation
for all those little things
you'd done right by me
so long ago; earliest memory

my first skating lesson,
a sunny winter afternoon
the nippy sense in my toes
as you laced me up, then
wobbly ankles and slipping blades
your steady hand
until you set me free
no looking back
So many other introductions,
all remind what you gave, and
now in absence mean so much more.
Preparation always in what you offered -
Dad, I so miss your
way of love

Robin Dyke

Birthday Cactus

The cactus my mother gave me,
grows anew
Sprightly fronds of Irish green
sprout from their elegant teal elders
Prickly and unassuming
nature's relentless cycle
growth nurses growth

Since her passing, the cactus
sustains her presence,
still nurtures this offsprung frond,
roots secure, so well tended
by her sure gardener's touch
Mother as nature's form -
my life in bloom from hers

Maui Ho'okahi

Warm fragrant air
Pure tropic light
Hues of emerald on
azure sea tinged surf
High volcanic slopes
valleys shadow deep
Maui –
each day as one
as no other

Dawn dresses in soft morning light
Birds sing, release the night
Sunbeams probe, bounce in unrest
Maui daybreak at its sublime best

Waving plumes of cane fields dance
capping views of green expanse
Distant spumes of sounding spray
signal whales in rapturous play
Polished shells dot solitary beaches
sweet plumeria probes inner reaches
Volcanic cones take clouds in tow
yet earth's fire bides presence just below

Robin Dyke

Kona winds usurp Trades' calms
building seas and bending palms
Nature plays to test your mettle
soon again all harsh storms settle
Land, sea and sky all converge
sooth away ambition's urge

Day's sun sinks behind Lanai
painting an expanse of vibrant sky
Then inky night drops as a veil
lit with bright stars as heaven's trail
Clear distant worlds so far for travel
one's speck of being an unfathomed marvel

Maui's unifying oneness
equals grace
gave Launiupoko as our place
heard our vows in open space

Ho'okahi under mid morning sun
to the day when breath is done
ashes on the cradling waves –
we return, as only one

Ho'okahi (ho'o-kă'-hi) **A oneness; a unity; to make one; a being only one.**

Plumeria

*The flower has no nectar duping its sphinx
moth pollinators*

Your flowers flutter from tree to ground
a scattering of starry gifts
petals of soft pastels
from center yellow into white
infant smooth, fragrance
subtle, delicate to the nose
Up close, so sweet -
light's call to the sphinx at night.
The disarming magic of nature's way
held within your shy un-nectared charm

Sure Thing

As if in liquid animation mode
joggers flow along the morning road
Early sun reflects arms and legs in motion
powers one world on its rotation
A likely sight as you can count on
like hunger in a refuge compound
Such is the balance of our globe
tipped to the niked on favoured road

Morning Mystery

On Maui mornings as I sit and write
An elderly couple regularly come in sight
Holding styrofoam cups of just plain white

They stride off purposely on the fairway grass
As if urgently bound on a crucial task
What is their morning mission? - I'd so like to ask

They look both ways to check their path
Straight across or around they do the math
So not to bring down any golfers' wrath

Their cups held out far from their lips
They seem so careful not to spill a drip
But never have I seen them even take one sip

Soon out of sight - where do they go?
Cups held uprightly, never low
Their bound for mission, will I ever know?

Wait! One morning I saw them coming back
But those styrofoam cups they both did lack
Apart from that, sadly - *I just don't know*

Robin Dyke

The Groundskeeper

Each morning
the leaves are raked
Each day
they fall to earth again

The tree of life, forever
shakes off its daily load
We as groundskeeper
dutifully gather
waiting for godot

Road to Hana

The 'heavenly' road to Hana is a bust
Take my word it's no sacred trust
Curve in, curve out, it never ends
Giving all encased neurotic bends
The views behold a spectacular coast
But one small skid and you all are toast
So many ways to take your lumps
On uneven pavement full of bumps
Few spots to safely stop and pause
Check the rental contract throw-up clause
Arriving finally at the Hasegawa General Store
Screams to stop! Please, no more, no more!
But mere more miles, say six to eight
And truly you will arrive at heaven's gate
There dashed all salvation that is sought
As the 'seven sacred pools' come to naught
Cascading elixir you thought to sip
Has long since diminished to a drip
All in all a most exhausting day
617 turns back to remake your way

Robin Dyke

Hana a pleasant village nothing more
Road survival t-shirts sold at the Store
Resist the purchase, don't look the jerk
The road to Hana is the devil's work

Lost Pair

Cast off on a rough shod road
lone and worn
a single flip-flop waits
(for what or who?)

How is it, one
of a matching pair
becomes estranged?

Does one foot
not follow
the other?

How do you abandon
your twin, after
so many steps shared?

How does one foot
stand to lose
grounding and support?

Perhaps one was thrown
into an encounter, or
wedged in a door as if a foot

Robin Dyke

Perhaps one stepped over
the edge or walked
a fine line

Or used to free
a kite from a tree
and took its place

Or serve as a prop
steps apart
to vary the landscape

Still - forlorn, displaced
inert and passing time
you as only the lonely
wait –
the flipped side of
a flopped relationship

Afternoon Delete

Tourists' thumbs flail the air
multi-tasking to who knows where
The here and now is not to bear
there's just not time to sit and stare
Sun, sand and sea can't compete
with text messages hypnotic bleat
One's own thoughts not to face as
dumb and dumber fill cyber space
Buy connection with a Wi-Fi fee
avoid small delight just to be
A smart phone devil with but one role
touch screen subversion of the soul

Robin Dyke

"We'll Take Care Of Martin Then ..."

She directed officiously,
into a cell phone
brushing past us
Weight of her world
against her ear
and on her lips
Eyes narrowed
to an urgent task
from which neither
Kaanapali trail
nor sea nor scene
could disconnect
Her partner
slouched along in tow
or was he –
in on the scheme
she was dealing?
And what of Martin -
demise, payoff, hospitality?
All gone with the
self-absorbed air
the moment of her passing

Tourist Bus

I join a shuttle queue
tourists who've had their shopping fill
Laughing, pushing we load on the bus
forced intimacy pressed to its hilt
With weary longing for my room
I shuffle in close synch along the aisle
a slow moving wave, that abruptly breaks
around a twisting traveller, wheel-chair bound
(an undertow to our aloha mood)
A tourist now felt trapped
my eyes glance at the boy
seek to engage yet can't reach out
My locked heart fumbles
while time in agonizing limbo drags
Finally a stop, passengers
a hasty retreating tide, surge off
And I? Mute and numb
Step off, and walk away

Devilish Passing

On the reverse façade of paradise
A topsy-turvy housing jumble -
what neighborhood is this?
On cue, an approaching grizzled figure
erect on a beat-up mo-ped
head capped in
bright magenta Arizona State hat
with iconic Sun Devil mascot
His faded singlet
and khaki shorts, face
devoid of expression,
all drab contrast to his hat
What of this man
- what of his hat?
How did they come to each other
- who's identity is whose?
Could he be alumnus (not likely)?
Was it the logo that appealed (for luck)?
Simply picked it from a rack at random (more likely)?
Or simply a discarded find -

the impish winking logo
a nosed thumb within the
old man's blank gaze as
he putts past

Robin Dyke

Fore What?

Where is the joy in awkward swing
that expects a ball to sweetly wing

One's spirits must find it rather tough
to spend all day out in the rough

Carts dart about for chip and putt
as players mainly rest on their butts

A handicap marks skill and ease
all equal though in paying green fees

While palpable exercise it might be called
such madness over one small ball

Tiki Taki

A *Tiki Bar* in name is quite enough
to wet tourist thirst for exotic stuff

Adding *Tiki* to the next door *Café*
the Polynesian theme starts to fray

Then *Tiki Restaurant* drums our heads
all hint of Tiki – now taki to be dread

Robin Dyke

Paradise Lost

With apologies to Joni Mitchell

We're paving paradise to no end
Like dominoes the concrete cascades
in instant malls, parking lots, rows on rows
No pristine shore to escape along
as sidewalks blanket once grassy ground
To no end we still have little clue
of what we had or what not to do
That big yellow taxi, a Prius now
took more away than your old man

December 31

Joggers endure
shuffle in their resolve
Walkers stride
in grim enjoyment
Golfers swing, groan and ah
wave from carts
Gardeners flirt
tidy what's out
of place
All the while the birds sing
to nothing in particular

Robin Dyke

Maui Lament

Life beguiles so tempting here
like sirens to Ulysses' ear

Time's wings set in steady beat
carpe diem does not repeat

Our footprints in the sand so fleeting
lost to the ocean of eternal seeking

Missing

This morning as I stirred
I sensed your presence -
your form
close as always
my world safe and right
Then full awake
only empty space
Cruel and true
I am so missing you

Robin Dyke

At Ease All Over Again

You call up to me
from the bottom of the stairs

Awakened sleep is all you wear
as you reach for my presence
in the silent house

Your innocence takes me back
to when we first slept together
and how you walked so naturally
unclothed into the room

Me under the sheets
still in my shorts
Quite a contrast
of ease and modesty

Precious is my image
of your curve of waist and hip
your beauty and your certainty
as you slipped into the bed

I marvel still
And here you are again
naked, looking up, no pretense

My awkward cover
falls away in ease
once more

Robin Dyke

Close Call

Can I hold you enough?
- the worrying theme of
my later days
Can a clock hold time?
Can a day hold its moments
or the light?
Can anything one treasures
last?
The terrible truth -
Nothingness
I can't imagine
the pain in its emptiness.
Could I go on -
without you?
What I can't imagine
compels my desperate
cling
All for the reassurance
of my arms
tight, around you

Rest Easy

What would you choose to play
for me, you wondered
Concern in your voice
uncertainty on your face
No comfort in my absent look
I too drew a blank
Nothing leapt out
from all the music shared
Only, it's not time -
the music will be there
soon enough

Robin Dyke

That We Might Be

No I would not give you false hope ...
Oh the mother and child reunion
Is only a moment away

– Paul Simon

As I walk along the edge
of the walled estates
dotting San Salvador's volcanic slopes
in the deep ravines
I find dark and narrow paths
lined with one-room shacks
held together
who knows how

I glimpse in
spot a young woman
child at her chest
Their faces bound in smile
attentive laughter
oblivious to my stare

Between their have not
and little else
                nothing
can dilute
the raw joy
of what they share

Robin Dyke

Revisiting Entre Pinos

The wall remains
always
Serenely
abruptly
a patient reminder
to confront
and learn
Move closer,
hear its call -
for you
to overcome
to live
to do necessary
and courageous acts
With and in support
of those bonded
forever
with the possible

Una Segunda Visita de Entre Pinos

El muro se queda
siempre
Tranquilo
abrupto, pero
una notificación paciente
para enfrentar
y aprender
Avanza
escucha su llamado -
para que tú
superes
vivas
hagas cosas
necesarias y valientes
Con y en apoyo de
esos lazos
para siempre
con lo posible

Robin Dyke

Schenley Night

*Schenley Distillers sponsored the annual
Canadian Football League most outstanding
player awards from 1953 until 1988*

Back in the fall of sixty
Three Cougars raw and brash
Rob Rube, John Mac, Tom Turkey
Showed up at a Grey Cup bash

Dressed in their champion blazers
Of junior football fame
All scrubbed and neatly polished
Three days before the Grey Cup game

Tom Senior provided entry
Courtesy of Dominion Stores
Perhaps with trepidation
Of what the invitation likely bore

The event was most prestigious
Next to the Grey Cup game
A brand of booze the sponsor
For three outstanding players to be named

The League's most outstanding player
Outstanding Canadian and lineman too
Jackie Parker was the favorite
Long forgot is who else was who

So keen the three as they arrived
Amidst the gathering throng
No wayward thoughts did they contrive
To suggest the evening might go wrong

The whiskey it was flowing
Schenley poured its very best
All but Tom were crowing
They were up to take the test

Many guests like them were hangers on
Hacks and has-beens quite a few
A hint of what's now called networking
Or, who the hell are you!

They mixed and mingled through the night
Chomped on the canapés
But Rob and John most enjoyed the bite
Of their Schenley's OFC's

Robin Dyke

At last the moment for awards
And the speeches all were made
Jackie Parker named most outstanding
His acceptance modest, drawled and staid

Now part of Schenley tradition
And figural to this tale to tell
Was a Tex Coulter oils rendition
Each winner received as well

Tex Coulter was an Alouette
A tackle who could opponents crush
But he also worked a pallet
And painted Schenley winners with a brush

Our boys milled and hero-worshipped
Once the awards were done
Jackie Parker autographed Rob's hankie
An A.E. Lee* cardboard one.

The ballroom soon was empty
The boys among the last
Only left were Tex's easeled portraits
With that a die serendipitously was cast

They hit the street quite happy
Well John and Rob at least
Thanks to Tom's good pappy
They'd had one dozer booze up feast!

The West Van bus was first to come
Tom and John got on
Rob waved them off, went to his stop
That's when the light went on

What lurks below the surface
What primal urge is fought
The Golden Fleece reveals its face
And the hunt is that what's sought

Back to the Hotel Vancouver Ballroom
Rob stealthily returned
Swept up the Parker portrait
To the rear exits then he turned

Down a backstairs stairwell
And out into a lane
Not a soul encountered
With Jackie still in-framed

With Schenley winner smothered
Deep beneath his coat
Heading north on Robson
On Schenley octane Rob did float

At Denman in a phone booth
Rob promptly made a call
To Tom the designated savior
Come help him with his haul

Tom responded swiftly
As enlightening he arrived
Not to take Rob homeward
But to return the heist back inside

Not purely moved by morals
Tom wore a worried look
Not for the threat of charges
But of Tom Senior on the hook

Back to Hotel Vancouver
Tom sped his downcast friend
Rob must return Jackie to his easel
On this he wouldn't bend

Back up the mezzanine stairway
To the ballroom without Dal**
Only two lonely Coulter portraits
Waiting for their troika pal

Jackie safely back in place
The wise completely unaware
Security was not lax you see
There just wasn't any there

So the evening ended
Without drama or recourse
A treasure only briefly lend-ed
By a Schenley liberating source

Now some schemes are predestined
And some are best forgot
Covert, overt, clandestine
Some learning here might be sought

Such is within this story's end
A moral to this tale:
A moment of regret averted
By the grace of a caring friend

* refers to a tuxedo rental store and the substitute breast pocket hankies
they gave away as a promotional item
** refers to Dal Richards, legionary big band orchestra leader, a fixture
at the Vancouver Hotel form 1940 to 1965.

Robin Dyke

Leaving

From holding on to letting go
... still digging for discoveries.

It ain't over till it's over.

- Yogi Berra

Remembering Neruda

We won't remember our dying
Neruda doesn't recall
writing that line
Curious
From nothing, to nothing
A life in between
No wonder hope so clings,
to the driftwood within
our drowning
reach

Robin Dyke

Teta Annie's Wish

I'm still here!
Her greeting
More question, than
declaration

A desperate *why*
help me understand
her pleading look

What more expected
when you remain
Two husbands and
your daughter –
god, your daughter!
- gone before

Life does not play fair
Older age brings
much more to bear
Wisdom cannot mitigate
the ache inside
that stays up late

Cast back to her urging
the three of four
who still remain
Recall how she took
your hands in hers
bid you promise
to come together
as you had
to keep this going!
after she was
gone

Did you think
Chrissy, or even you
would be first?

The promise
down to you three
is still here!

Robin Dyke

Juxtaposition

Beside the hotel pool, tourists sprawl
corralled together row on row
Laughing shapes, sizes and ages all
devoted flock to a burning god
oblivious to next door's barren ground
where markers, crosses stare like ghosts
Adults, children splash no more
sunless, silent six feet down

Pinball

Single player, racked up load
shooting thoughts that just don't hold
His synaptic hits like pinball strikes
careen off each other and the like
while psychic flippers wildly flail
striking out at what isn't there
Back and forth his memory shifts
without *have I told you this?* hint of tilt
Pinball wizard or curtained Oz –
what drives his longings to no end?
What can I say or do to bring a pause
that might lead to ease or rest within?
Bing, ding, ping the score resets
serves up yet another replay game

Robin Dyke

Breaks

How she hates the state she's in
falling not just once, but hard down twice
Shattering a hip along with aging dreams
replacement joint skewed up her stance
Left to shuffle, drag a shorter leg along
not quite sure where she belongs
All her escapes flown off with hope
even preparing meals not in her scope
Dependent now for so many needs
irritant exchanges with those adored
Not the way she saw her final years
bite her lip, hold back the tears
Small pleasures make sitting seem less long;
a country drive or her hair being permed
Or as Agatha Christie and whodunit cast
with plots to unravel her mind runs free
Yet back in the present with best friend past
releasing talks gone as well (*I miss her so!*)
-- how she hates the state she's fallen to

Opening

Eerie silence
surrounds the deserted house
The lock has tightened
its grip on the thick
and weathered door
closing off all within –
yet, an inquiring twist
of the rusted knob
might spring its dark
ghost free

Robin Dyke

Rest Home

Solitary beside her bed
back to the door
face to the window
a book cradled in her lap
Surprised by my touch
silver hair frames blue eyes
that search to know me
until her smile connects us
Exclaims my name, in our embrace
I feel her fragile state
News she wants, her questions
answered, asked again
Of her needs or inner thoughts, few clues:
I've had a good life
I have all I need – a little more
No secrets, always just one regret
if only the cat
had not tripped me up -
this broken hip!
I dare to ask; what then?
Yet I pause, as reflection slips
with the moment across her face

Time to go she bids
Mine or hers I wonder
Waves affection with her mother's look
I love you and *I love you too* -
back to the altar of her book

Robin Dyke

Lust Lost

The sun moves low
across a barren sky of age
faded and worn

Spring's once fresh promise
but feigning stir

Summer's humid wind gone fall

Flamed and crowned
the longing shadow's cry
of winter's settling in

The sun moves low …

Life Compounded

Canadian woman killed in Georgia gator attack

News item

Lush gated Georgian grounds
a safe haven for reclining years
Controlled, patrolled, protected
from harm's way or wild surprise

So began her day as those before
routine lived out, no thought of more
No need for extraordinary care
time to walk the lagoon shore

She must have had an inkling
just before the gator struck
The surface water oh so gently breaking
she'd used up eighty-three years of luck

A foot seized tight within its jaws
the beast dragged her towards the slough
She thrashed, her life flashed
believing it was most likely through

Despite doom's lock on hope's last stand
she fought as fiercely as she could
Lost pummeling fists to those mean teeth
- in do-or-die to wrest her snared foot free

Within the murk and ghostly swamp
the gator had cruel control
Pulled her deep into the silt abyss
a reptilian nightmare took its toll

Next morning, spotted floating free
her stumped arms and leg sedate
Markers to the path of unanticipated risks
where dark creatures hold our fate

So, who's to know how we will go?
In our beds we trust - yet
no sure choices direct fate's means
All can be said: life will end.

Nothing Left

If love goes
whatever would be left
but lifeless chill and lows
If love goes
the flowers wither
all is empty and bereft
If love goes
nothing surely could be left

Robin Dyke

Shady Creek

I linger at the churchyard
as afternoon's long shadows
draw across the dead
Who stirs below?
Who might even wonder?
On the white steeple tower
the fading winter sun
glints off the silent bell

Left

*One's remaining image, that unique way of
being and doing, left in the minds of others,
continues to act upon them – in anecdote,
reminiscence, dream; as exemplar, mentor-
ing voice, ancestor – a potent force working
in those with lives left to live.*

- James Hillman

Isn't it grand boys, to be bloody well dead!

- Clancy Brothers Folk Song

Surfacing

Picture this: beyond our days
archeologists from another world
probe for insights in the ground -
what of who passed here?

Along the paths and highways of our routes
they lightly scrape, brush away to reveal
strewn trails of cigarette butts, rusted bottle caps
lipped with the DNA of our discarding ways
Life's deep questions scattered absently -
as bread-crumb-poised answers
never to be found

Robin Dyke

Arrogance

Custer stood his ground
to make his fight
Caught, surprised
amidst wild swirling fate
Golden strands that once
drew so much light
Dead and caked
in blood stained dirt

What You Wear

Che was a scruffy, bearded
do good fool
An iconic image
for some reason that's still cool
The workers of the world
he thought he'd save
all long abandon aside
his desolate, Bolivian grave

Robin Dyke

Mollusk Pollock

"What does the painting mean?"

- Jackson Pollock

The sidewalk smear confronted
A surrealist streak played out
An abstract trail of slither
A glob of slug unbound

Slick track completely random
Dripped along its concrete roam
Was the mucus mollusk even thinking
So beyond its lush leaf home

The end expressed so slowly
A drying out of mark and time
Spent and stuck forlornly
Last vestige a line of slime

Modern impressionism or pure chaos
What sluggish message drawn
Why ever did it venture
So beyond its lush leaf home

The King Is Dead, Long Live The King

February 25, 2003 - John MacMillan Stirling
Lecky passed away this week. Lecky was a
well rounded individual, successful en-
trepreneur, philanthropist, as well as a
Canadian Olympic Rowing Team medalist.

John Lecky dead
At 62!
Sudden
Big Man on Campus done
Just like that
It's over
That's all there is
For *him*
What ever could have flashed
as life turned dim
for this *tall, imposing figure* and his
infectious sense of fun?

So abrupt an end
how could this be!
He was a king

at least he seemed
His birth and touch of gold
invincible
A dominating force
beyond my grasp
of self-conscious worth

Time elapsed
like a curtain drawn
between the pedestal I saw
and death's quick call
Yet I remain -
what of that?
Perhaps the upper hand of fate
- but wait
the King did live
and live within his time
Take that away
as the reflection clears
on my obscure sense of self back then
Envy of what seemed beyond
My folly of resentful youth

Could I have seen it then -
the message timed for now
John Lecky does live on

Frank

11.08.39 – 28.12.06

Frank loved to run, was trim and fit
Full of life lived and yet to come
Least expecting that's when it hit
Two years fighting his run was done

Full of life lived and yet to come
Courage and humor set his pace
Two years fighting his run was done
Crossed the line that ends our race

Courage and humor set his pace
Running against a menacing wind
Crossed the line that ends his race
Hit the wall we can't rescind

Pressing wearily against the wind
Least expected that's when we hit
The looming wall we can't rescind
Frank loved to run, was trim and fit

Robin Dyke

Life:Art

Your art altered self -
how much was you?
(*Really*, who?)

Your aptitude to draw
fated you to art -
but what stroke struck
your choice of what and how?
And, of your thoughts, what
did they paint across your mind?
(These I never drew from you)

The pigment mix, what did it bring
as you gave watercolor birth
to a landscape scene?
(Bore me a felt connection)

Prolific, in demand, the shows and sales -
brought you what?
(Were you drawn at all to express
love in any way to me?)

Then, some limit reached, you
abruptly stopped -
lay down your brush to
paint no more.
(Could I expect attention then?
- Not to be explored)

The canvas of your life
framed and walled
blank and tight

Robin Dyke

Black & White Photo

Circa Winter 1940

Your smile is for me
From your arms, I look out
to a wondrous world
no sense of distant threat
Matching parkas frame
our faces with snow white rabbit fur
I seem about to laugh
while you gaze
understated in trim glamour -
curls of subtle coiffured hair
eyebrows highlighted slightly
a hint of lipstick
So much the camera caught
Love openly exposed
before seven decades flash -
to a mood of sepia being cast
Now I hold you, stroke your hair
white and soft as that fine rabbit trim
I sponge your brow, look

for connection in your vacant eyes
a mirror to the threshold on which you pose
Silence as you slip away
color seeps to black and white

Robin Dyke

Saint Peter

October 1941 – December 2012
Who we gona' call ... now?

The Christmas songs lament
the darkness of your passing
Bells struck mute
lights less bright
your playful smile gone out

Breeze in - be gone
bombast in both directions
No idle worth
just standing still
Move on - no hesitation

Hey, what's happening?!
your eyebrow-punctuated-entrance
Unabashed your questions asked,
resistance charmed within the spell
of your effervescent pestering

Those unexpected times you'd drop by
brought nights of such sweet havoc -
the drink, the tales, the laughter!
Last visit as babe you crawled
and curled asleep beneath our table

Loyal had no greater marker as a friend -
be there for others in a flash
stick by them was your virtue
Even brush with death towards the end
could not deter the beat of your commitment

And, *don't look back*
your forward guiding mantra
Could you have heard
death's approaching gait
catching up before the finish?

Now who will stand for friends in need?
Yes, who indeed? The memories of
your quick and ready presence
give voice to your ever living character –
in saint and devilish ways you were and will always be

Isn't it grand boys, to be bloody well dead!

Robin Dyke

Lean in: A Postscript

The source of the journey is the mystery

I gained optimism from my mother who was open to the ways
and mysteries of the world. She found solace in rewriting
found lines of text or a poem on scraps of paper she tucked
away in private but scattered locations. She delighted in
unexpected surprise endings. My dad had a darker view of the
world, black or white – little tolerance for the ambiguity my
mother could flow with. He sought order and symmetry, neatly
packaged and labeled. As for me, I favor my mother's wonder
with bits of my dad's love of structure seeping in as the views
and organization of this collection may suggest. The poems all
began on their own, no particular theme being followed other
than preoccupation of the moment. Once the collection ex-
isted the themes of *Lasting, Leaving and Left* popped out as the
topics or tasks that in reflection seem behind my verses (and
my age and stage of this ride we are all on). There is at least
one further *L* and that is the big one of having *Lived* fully, well
before we *Leave*.

About the Author

Robin Dyke is a connector.
Poetry is an extension of his work
as a consultant and educator,
bringing to attention what gives
meaning and joy. Robin and his
wife Marline, live in Cordova
Bay, Vancouver Island.